CAREC TRANSPORT STRATEGY 2030 MIDTERM REVIEW

MARCH 2026

ASIAN DEVELOPMENT BANK

ADB

6 ADB Avenue, Mandaluyong City, 1550 Metro Manila, Philippines
Tel +63 2 8632 4444; Fax +63 2 8636 2444
www.adb.org

ISBN 978-92-9277-684-8 (print); 978-92-9277-685-5 (PDF); 978-92-9277-686-2 (ebook)
Publication Stock No. TCS260048-2
DOI: http://dx.doi.org/10.22617/TCS260048-2

Note:
In this publication, "$" refers to United States dollars.

Cover design by Mike Cortes.

CONTENTS

TABLE, FIGURES, AND MAPS

Table

Figures

Maps

ABBREVIATIONS

ADB	Asian Development Bank
BCP	border crossing point
CAREC	Central Asia Regional Economic Cooperation
CITA	CAREC Integrated Trade Agenda
COVID-19	coronavirus disease
CPMM	Corridor Performance Measurement and Monitoring
CTS	CAREC Transport Strategy
MTR	midterm review
PRC	People's Republic of China
WHO	World Health Organization

EXECUTIVE SUMMARY

The Central Asia Regional Economic Cooperation (CAREC) Transport Strategy 2030 was endorsed by CAREC ministers in November 2019, and this midterm review (MTR) follows the recent MTR of the overall CAREC Strategy 2030. This MTR was designed to reflect global, regional, and national developments that have occurred since its inception, including factors such as climate risks, digital transformation, and shifting geopolitical dynamics. It was undertaken in conjunction with CAREC member countries to ensure that it reflected their objectives and demands for regional transport services and their ability to deliver intended outcomes in each of the transport subsectors. Consultations also involved development partners, private sector stakeholders, and the CAREC Institute.

To reflect the important synergies between transport, trade, and digitalization, the MTR was undertaken in conjunction with midterm reviews for both the CAREC Integrated Trade Agenda (CITA) 2030 and the CAREC Digital Strategy 2030.

The key findings are that the CAREC Transport Strategy 2030 (CTS) has successfully delivered improvements in its two strategic objectives, connectivity and sustainability, and continues to be relevant. Its five strategic pillars comprising (i) cross-border transport and logistics facilitation, (ii) roads and road asset management, (iii) road safety, (iv) railways, and (v) aviation should also continue to provide the basis of the strategic framework. To reflect changing development needs the MTR introduces a third strategic objective, namely, resilience to mitigate disruptions from a changing external operational environment.

The MTR's four key recommendations are:

1. **Strengthen Cross-Border Transport and Corridor Efficiency**
   - Establish financing facility for border crossing point (BCP) improvements addressing infrastructure and soft-side needs and promote joint BCPs;
   - Promote economic corridor approach to comprehensively address transport connectivity, accessibility, and mobility; remove bottlenecks; and enhance economic activities along corridors;

- Enhance capacity and connectivity of Corridor 2 through infrastructure upgrades, multimodal logistics hubs, harmonized regulations, and digital processes; and
- Address bottlenecks in Caspian Sea transport and Black Sea ports by expanding port capacity and multimodal connection.

2. **Promote Modal Diversification and Smart Mobility**
   - Strengthen intermodal connectivity, especially among ports, railways, and roads to boost efficiency and lower logistics costs;
   - Encourage policy frameworks supporting modal shift to low-carbon transport options such as railway and waterborne transport;
   - Assist with logistics process harmonization and propose regional standards for multimodal documentation; and
   - Launch the Smart Mobility Working Group to promote intelligent transport systems, transport digitalization, e-mobility, comprehensive public transport development, and sustainable urban planning.

3. **Scale Up Green, Resilient, Inclusive, and Digitalized Transport**
   - Include resilience as one of the strategic objectives of the CTS alongside connectivity and sustainability;
   - Support greening and electrification of transport (e.g., Green Roads Tool Kit) and creating low-emission zones in urban areas to support the nationally determined contribution targets;
   - Broaden road safety efforts by adopting the safe system approach and enhancing digital solutions; and
   - Promote sustainable logistics practices and integrate trade-related digital platforms for international freight operators.

4. **Deepen Institutional Collaboration and Future Planning**
   - Enhance CAREC Institute's functions on transport and economic corridor planning, policy advice, and capacity building scaling up the function for Corridor Performance Measurement and Monitoring (CPMM);
   - Regularly organize the Smart Mobility, Road, and Railway working groups under the Transport Sector Coordinating Committee and strengthen the link with trade facilitation bodies on the CITA and CAREC Digital Strategy;
   - Prepare annual transport sector profile and flagship reports utilizing Asian Transport Observatory and CPMM; and
   - Plan for post-2030 needs: trade shifts, climate risks, and tech disruptions.

The MTR recommends that the CAREC Institute take an increasing role in the development of the region's transport sector through undertaking important technical studies, research, and assessments in line with its capacity. Before the end of the CTS 2030 period, the region's transport needs should be assessed to identify priority needs for the sector beyond 2030.

Chapter I

INTRODUCTION

1. The Central Asia Regional Economic Cooperation (CAREC) Transport Strategy 2030 (CTS 2030) was endorsed by CAREC ministers in November 2019.[1] It was prepared considering the overarching CAREC 2030 Strategy, which provided the framework for fostering regional cooperation and integration across the 11 countries in the region.[2] The midterm review (MTR) of the overarching CAREC 2030 Strategy[3] was endorsed by the CAREC ministers in November 2024. One of its key recommendations was to launch MTRs of all sector strategies to ensure their alignment with the overall regional strategy by reviewing their effectiveness and recalibrating their focus where deemed necessary. In line with this recommendation, this report summarizes the findings of the MTR of CTS 2030.

2. The MTR of CTS 2030 was conducted in partnership with CAREC countries through an extensive program of country visits that included workshops with a broad range of stakeholders from both the public and private sectors, and individual meetings with key agencies representing ministries of finance, economic planning, and the technical line ministries representing the transport, trade, and digital sectors, among others.[4] The outputs from the country consultations provided the core information for refining the strategy. This was combined with changing priorities attributable to global events and technological developments, which helped to identify the various measures that were needed to sharpen the effectiveness of the strategy and define appropriate adjustments that would deliver improved outcomes and impacts in the transport sector over the remainder of the period to 2030 and beyond.

3. Transport has been a major component of CAREC investment. During the CTS 2030 period 2021–2024, $8.61 billion worth of investments were made, comprising 16.5% of total CAREC investments. Of the total $3.91 billion invested in transport

1 Asian Development Bank (ADB). 2020. *CAREC Transport Strategy 2030*.

2 CAREC comprises Afghanistan, Azerbaijan, Georgia, Kazakhstan, the Kyrgyz Republic, Mongolia, Pakistan, People's Republic of China, Tajikistan, Turkmenistan, and Uzbekistan. ADB placed its regular assistance in Afghanistan on hold effective 15 August 2021 and this midterm review did not incorporate the views of the country.

3 ADB. 2024. *CAREC 2030 Strategy Midterm Review*.

4 The CTS 2030 MTR country consultation program included meetings and workshops held on 11–14 February 2025 in Mongolia, 5–7 March 2025 with CAREC National Focal Points in the Philippines, 11–13 March 2025 in Kazakhstan, 17–20 March 2025 in the People's Republic of China, 4–8 April 2025 in Azerbaijan, 10–11 April 2025 in the Kyrgyz Republic, 21–25 April 2025 in Uzbekistan, 28–29 April 2025 in Tajikistan, 6–7 May 2025 in Georgia (virtual), 16 May 2025 in Turkmenistan (virtual), and 2–3 June 2025 in Pakistan. Draft recommendations were presented at a side event of 2025 Summit of the International Transport Forum on 21 May 2025.

by development partners, $2.13 billion (54.5%) was financed by the Asian Development Bank (ADB), $1.22 billion (31.2%) by other development partners, and $0.56 billion (14.4%) by CAREC countries. These investments greatly contributed to enhancing connectivity among CAREC countries and boosting international trade and transport.

4. CTS 2030 also incorporated individual sub-strategies for two of the modal themes, notably the railway sector and road safety.[5] The MTR incorporated a review of both these sub-strategies to ensure that their focus continued to be in line with overall CAREC objectives in the transport sector and their ability to deliver the intended outcomes in each of their subsectors.

5. Transport is an essential service that is highly correlated to other sectors in the economy since it provides important linkages between production and consumption locations and facilitates economic growth and development. For this reason, transport and trade are closely interconnected; transport provides the means for facilitating trade and without efficient transport, the economic benefits of trade are unlikely to reach their full potential. Digital transformation is rapidly changing a whole range of activities across the development spectrum and particularly impacts the way in which both the transport and trade sectors affect the delivery of infrastructure and services. Digitalization is revolutionizing transport infrastructure and services leading to more efficient, safer, and sustainable mobility solutions. An important interaction between transport and trade is the extension of paperless processes and procedures to facilitate transport of freight across borders more efficiently, i.e., reducing time and delays. The extension of digitization in the CAREC region is expected to have a profound impact on increasing the efficiency of intraregional and external trade and raise the importance of the arterial multimodal transport corridors serving the region.

6. To reflect the important synergies between transport, trade, and digitalization, the MTR was undertaken in conjunction with the MTRs for both the CAREC Integrated Trade Agenda (CITA) 2030 and CAREC Digital Strategy 2030.[6] This action is expected to broaden the scope of potential support to the transport sector by incorporating elements of trade and digital structures in the scope of future projects and programs thereby leveraging benefits across all sectors.

7. The MTR also acknowledged the findings and conclusions of the recent review of the development effectiveness of the CAREC program.[7]

5 ADB. 2017. *Unlocking the Potential of Railways: A Railway Strategy for CAREC, 2017–2030*; and ADB. 2017. *Safely Connected: A Regional Road Safety Strategy for CAREC Countries, 2017–2030*.

6 ADB. 2019. *CAREC Integrated Trade Agenda 2030 and Rolling Strategic Action Plan 2018–2020*; and ADB. 2022. *CAREC Digital Strategy 2030: Accelerating Digital Transformation for Regional Competitiveness and Inclusive Growth*.

7 ADB. 2025 (forthcoming). *CAREC 2030 Development Effectiveness: 2021–2023*.

Chapter II

TRANSPORT AND TRADE FACILITATION

A. Synergies Between Transport and Trade

8. Multiple studies have identified the synergies between transport and trade.[8] Efficient trade is a key parameter for achieving economic development. Perhaps the most important driver of trade is the availability of transport services, as trade relies heavily on efficient, reliable, resilient, and safe transport to move goods, services, and people between origins and destinations. Transport infrastructure and accompanying logistics services provide the framework for international trade to connect businesses with international markets and foster economic development. Efficient low-cost transport services are essential in the CAREC region, which is largely landlocked, with vast distances linking its countries to many of its internal and external trading partners. A consequence of the region's geographical location is that the long distances to major markets add significant transport time and costs to traded goods and services, and this alone provides a considerable barrier to trade and foreign investment compared to countries and locations in other regions. It is therefore critical that transport services in the region are low-cost, efficient, and reliable. Since the availability of quality transport infrastructure is a major requirement to nurture economic growth and development in the region, the support provided under the CAREC program has prioritized the development of transport infrastructure and services, which comprised 68% of overall investment as of end-2024 (Figure 1).

8 See e.g., United Nations Conference on Trade and Development (UNCTAD) Secretariat. 2003. *Efficient Transport and Trade Facilitation to Improve Participation by Developing Countries in International Trade*.

Figure 1: CAREC Investment by Sector
(as of December 2024)

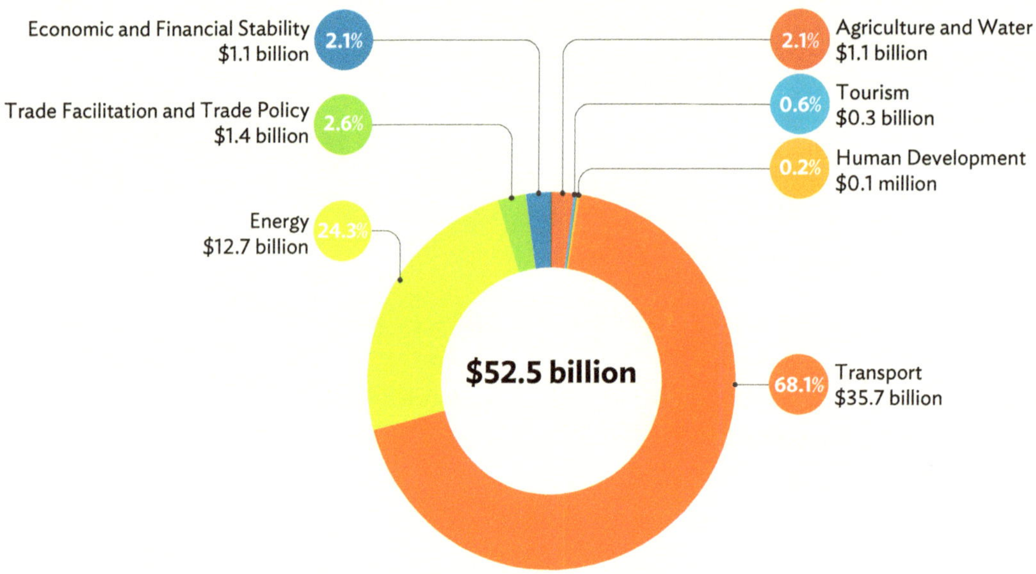

CAREC = Central Asia Regional Economic Cooperation.
Note: The CAREC portfolio (investment projects) database is undergoing review and verification in consultation with development partners and the CAREC sector focal in the Asian Development Bank.
Source: CAREC Secretariat.

B. Recent Trends in Trade in the CAREC Region

9. Since the adoption of the CTS in 2019, merchandise trade in the region has increased rapidly (Figure 2), despite the global economic downturn caused by the coronavirus disease (COVID-19) pandemic. Over the 5-year period from 2018 to 2023, total trade turnover in the CAREC region as a whole increased by 52%, which compares favorably with the global trade volume increase of 22%. However, if trade in energy is excluded from the analysis, the increase in goods and services for the region reached 60%. This achievement is attributed to both robust growth in the CAREC economies as well as the ability of individual CAREC country economies to fill gaps in the Russian market created after the Russian invasion of Ukraine with exports and re-exports. The notable features of trade with respect to their impact on transport services is that a high proportion of exports comprises extractive industry products, such as hydrocarbons, minerals, and agricultural products, while the bulk of imports consists of manufactured products. Hydrocarbon exports are primarily transported by pipelines while merchandise products primarily use road and railway services. Overall, there is a large trade imbalance between non-energy imports and exports in many CAREC economies. Similar imbalance is also observed in the region's transit trade, where export volumes from the People's Republic of China (PRC) are significantly greater than the imports from trading partners.

Figure 2: Changes in the Structure of Merchandise Trade in CAREC Economies, 2018–2030

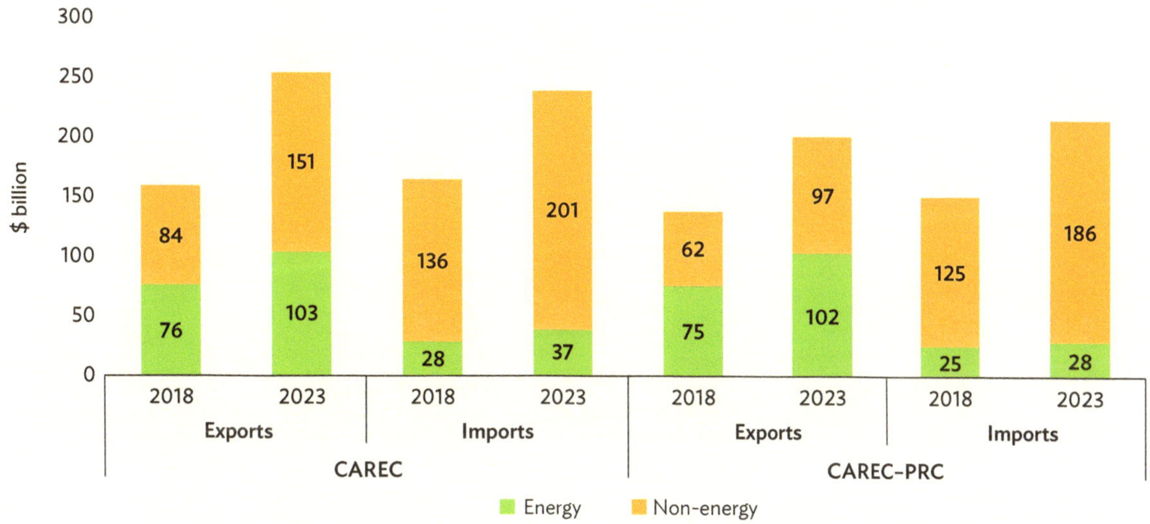

CAREC = Central Asia Regional Economic Cooperation, PRC = People's Republic of China.
Note: PRC data are for Xinjiang Uyghur Autonomous Region and Inner Mongolia Autonomous Region only.
Source: UN Comtrade; and national statistics and customs agencies.

10. Progress in trade diversification during 2018–2023 was limited. CAREC is a relatively minor trading partner for the PRC, although its role increased over the period to reach 2.2% of total trade turnover in 2023, compared to 1.5% in 2018. Trade patterns in the region are dominated by the PRC, which is the primary trading partner of each of the other CAREC economies. Mongolia and Pakistan have limited trade with the economies of the Caucasus and Central Asia and with each other. Central Asian economies have three main trade partners: the PRC, the Russian Federation, and the European Union (EU). Trade between the key external markets as well as intra-CAREC trade increased by about 10% a year over the 5-year period (Figure 3).

11. The countries of the CAREC region are geographically located between the major markets of East Asia to the east, the European Union to the west, and the Russian Federation to the north. The region is well known for its trade and transit corridors, which historically linked the "Silk Road" route between east and west, serving as a major trading corridor for many centuries. The major trade corridors traverse each of the Central Asian and Caucasus countries and provide vital links to external markets for the landlocked countries of the region. Today, the region is still known for its trade facilitation role and provides important transit routes linking major transcontinental markets. Due to its geographical location and size, Kazakhstan is the main transit country catering to trade flows in both the east–west and north–south directions. Transit trade via Kazakhstan can be characterized by the volumes of containerized traffic carried by the country's railway system (Figure 4). Traffic demand has more than doubled over 2018–2023, reflecting significant growth during the COVID-19 pandemic and especially since the Russian invasion of Ukraine

Figure 3: Merchandise Trade Turnover with Key Trade Partners, 2018–2023

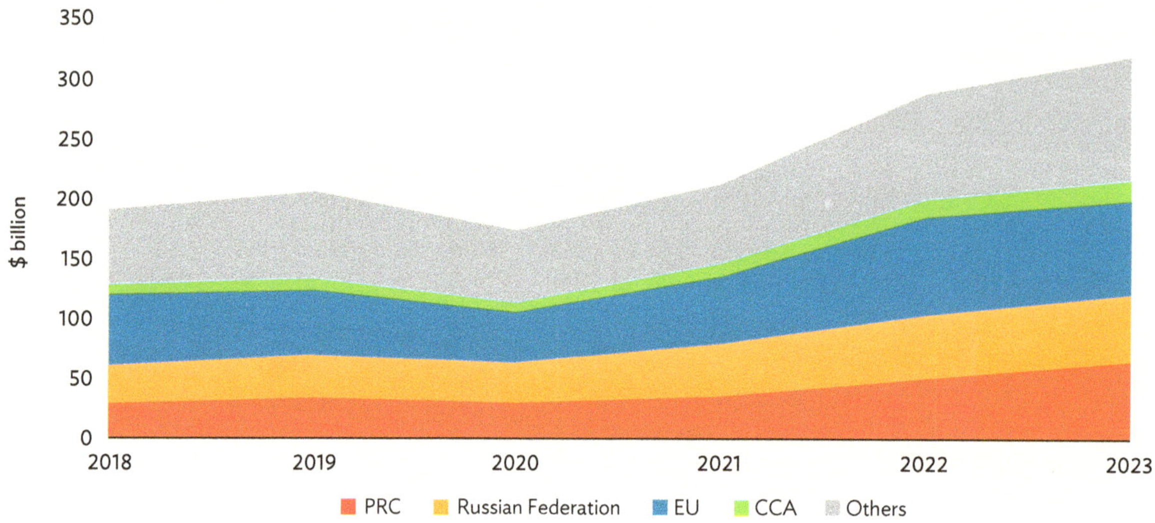

CCA = Caucasus and Central Asia, EU = European Union, PRC = the People's Republic of China.
Sources: UN Comtrade; and national statistical and customs agencies.

Figure 4: International Container Transit via Kazakhstan, 2018–2023

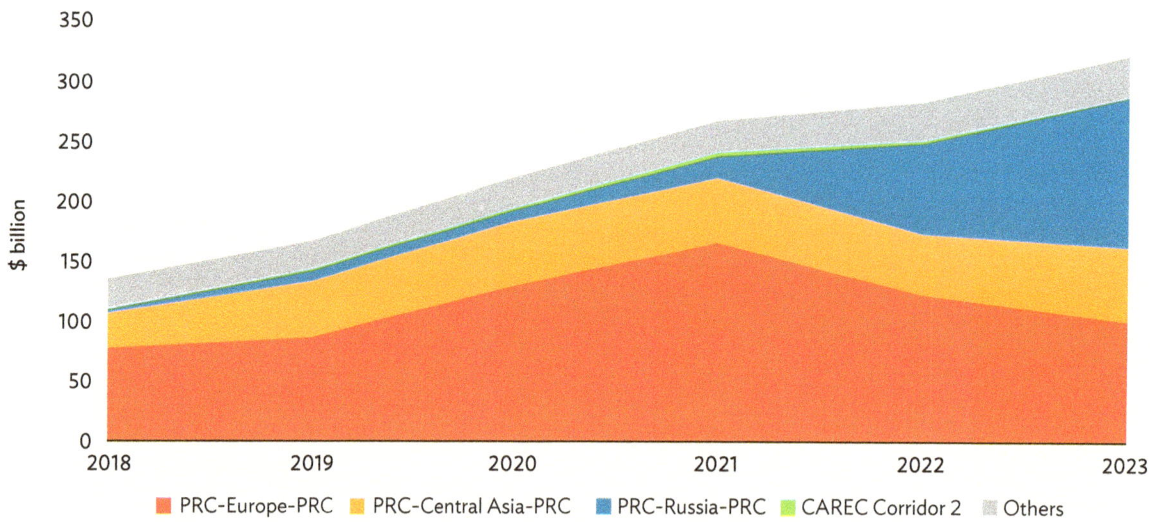

CAREC = Central Asia Regional Economic Cooperation, PRC = People's Republic of China, TEU= twenty-foot equivalent unit.
Note: "Other" includes flows between Russian Federation (both European part and Far East) and Central Asia, PRC and Belarus, etc.
Source: National railway company, Kazakhstan Temir Zholy.

as trade between the PRC and Russian Federation has increased sharply. The volumes of containers reflect the main trading routes linking East Asia with the Russian Federation and the EU, and although considerably smaller in volume, trade between Central Asia and East Asia is growing, albeit slowly. Azerbaijan also serves as a transit trade hub in the region although significantly smaller in volume. In 2024, the Port of Baku (Alat) handled more than 70,000 containers, of which about 34% arrived from the adjacent ports of Kazakhstan. Cargo traffic volumes across the Caspian Sea increased significantly compared to the same period in the previous year, with a 6.7% increase recorded.[9] The capacity and climatic limitations associated with the waterborne transport services and port–rail interconnections for trans-Caspian trade are significant challenges to unlocking greater use of the CAREC Corridor 2.

12. Some CAREC countries report trade data by transport mode. While energy flows of oil and gas primarily use pipelines, non-energy trade mainly uses railway, road, and waterborne transport for trans-Caspian Sea and onward transport from Black Sea ports in Georgia to continental Europe. Figure 5 illustrates the 2022 modal data reported from four CAREC countries that have considerably different economies and rely to a different extent on railway or road transport. In Kazakhstan, with its vast distances, railways have a dominant role in the transport of exports and imports, while in the mountainous Kyrgyz Republic road transport is more dominant. Waterborne transport, a relatively minor mode, is used in Kazakhstan for trans-Caspian movements while in Georgia, which has access to the Black Sea, it is used for less than half of its trade. A common feature of trade in many countries is the dominance in volumes of imports compared to the volume of exports for merchandise trade. A similar imbalance is also a key characteristic of East Asia–EU trade, where exports from East Asia dominate. A less observed cost of trade imbalances is the logistics cost associated with empty containers needing relocation to demand locations.

13. Trade in services (measured by $) increased faster than trade in physical goods in many CAREC economies for 2018–2023 (Figure 6). This growth was due to an increase in tourism and other international movements of people and, in some countries, an increase in financial flows and information and communication technology services. Transport and travel services are the two main components of trade in services, with a high proportion of trade in services attributable to tourism. In CAREC economies, trade in transport services typically constitutes between 30% and 40% of total trade in services while the proportion of travel services amounts to between 20% and 30% of the total. An important difference is that travel services have a high dependence on the aviation sector, while trade in goods is primarily dependent on road and rail transport. With respect to trade in financial and

[9] With respect to the modal capacity of the alternative trade routes serving the PRC to Europe trade, the capacity of Corridor 2 (largely coinciding with the Middle Corridor) is estimated at 75,000 twenty-foot equivalent units (TEUs) which compares to 1,575,000 TEUs for the northern corridor and more than 35 million TEUs for sea routes, according to details provided in a presentation by an ADB port and logistics consultant to the 19th Transport Sector Coordinating Committee, Almaty, Kazakhstan, October 2022.

information and communication technology services, the availability of digital hard and soft infrastructure is of most importance. Of increasing importance is the role of digital technologies in fostering increased efficiencies and lower costs of transport and logistics services.

Figure 5: Non-Energy Trade by Transport Mode for Select CAREC Economies, 2022

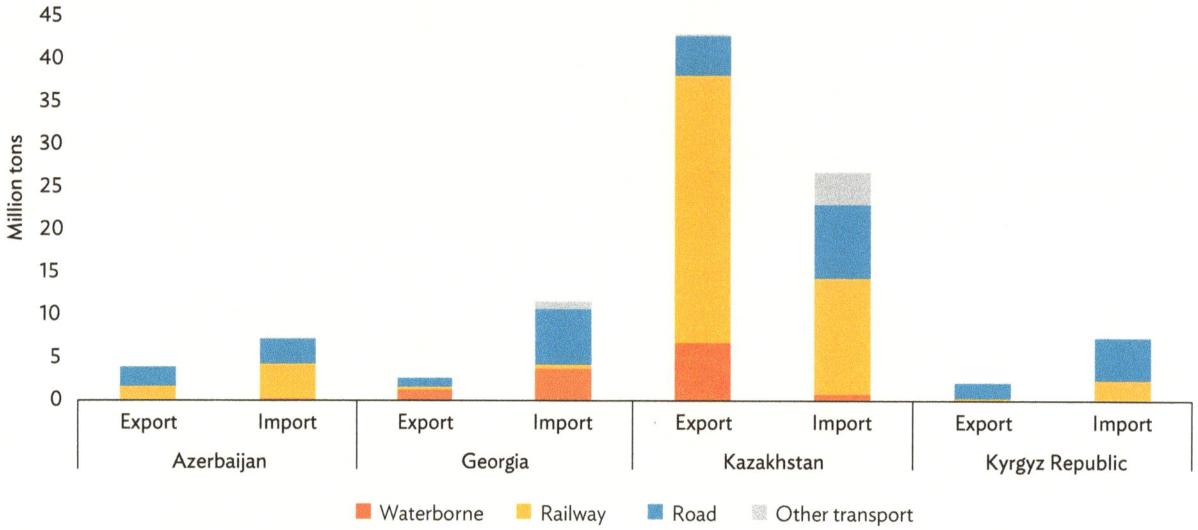

CAREC = Central Asia Regional Economic Cooperation.
Source: UN Comtrade.

Figure 6: Growth of Trade in Services for Select CAREC Economies, 2018–2023

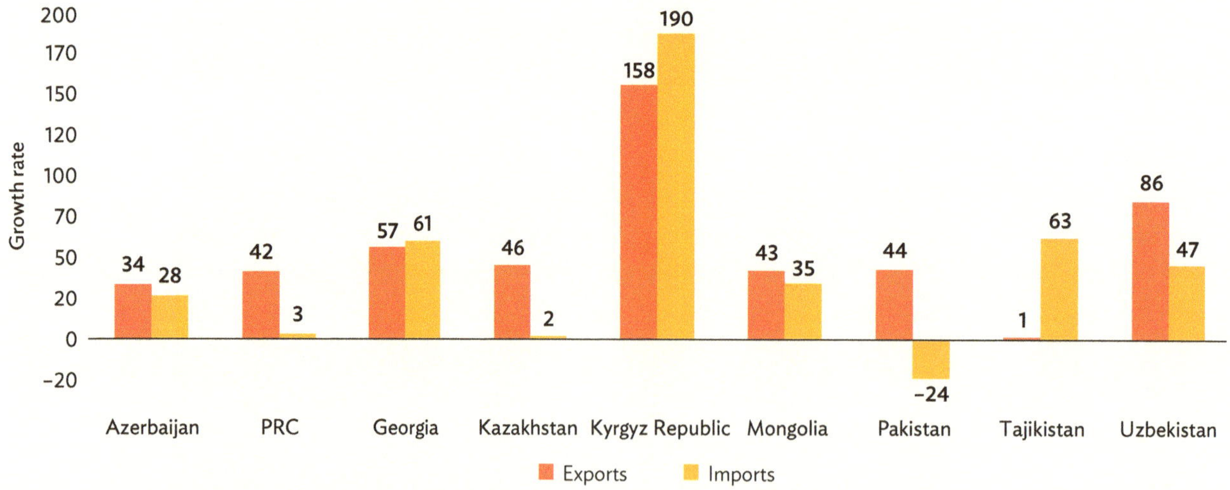

CAREC = Central Asia Regional Economic Cooperation, PRC = People's Republic of China.
Sources: Central banks of the CAREC economies.

Chapter III

GLOBAL DEVELOPMENTS AND CHANGING TECHNOLOGIES

A. Introduction

14. Since the drafting and approval of the CTS in 2019, the world has undergone a number of developments that have significantly impacted the way in which the transport sector is viewed from a developmental perspective, while technological changes have resulted in rapid changes to the way transport services are operated and delivered. In this respect, policymakers implementing the CTS need to be aware not only of the changing global environment but also the new technologies and processes that are changing the demand for, and use of, transport infrastructure and services. Global conflicts can also have a major effect on the demand for, and delivery of, transport services, and the CAREC region has been impacted by such events. The CTS needs to provide appropriate support to ensure projects and programs address climate risks, decarbonization and greening targets, and utilization of digital technologies. In addition, increased resilience needs to be built into transport infrastructure and services to accommodate future risks.

B. Climate Resilience, Disaster Prevention, and Decarbonization

15. The CAREC region is highly susceptible to climate impacts, including rising temperatures, extreme weather events, and unforeseen disasters triggered by natural hazards, all of which are expected to increase.[10] The transport sector helps integrate the economy by providing links between centers of economic production and markets both within the region and externally. As such, it is important that potential disruptions to transport services are minimized by reducing risks and increasing the resilience of infrastructure. Storms and floods expose transport infrastructure and services to increased risks. Rising temperatures will damage road pavements, buckle railroad tracks, and reduce the depth of the Caspian Sea, all of which will impact the operation of transport. Even where physical damage is not apparent, climate impacts will likely decrease productivity of transport operations and affect users' safety and comfort.

10 ADB. 2024. *Central Asia Regional Economic Cooperation Program Climate Change Action Plan 2025–2027*.

It is therefore important to implement measures to mitigate climate risks by increasing the resilience of transport infrastructure networks and services to deal with, adapt, and recover from possible disruptions.

16. Decarbonizing transport is a major global policy thrust designed to attain a low-carbon economy and has been recognized in several individual CAREC countries' nationally determined contributions. The transport sector is responsible for about a quarter of global carbon dioxide emissions, making it a major contributor to the changing climate. As a result, transport has a key role in the transition to a low-carbon economy, and the sector is exposed to a number of transition risks. New developments are likely to affect the transport sector through various channels, such as increased carbon pricing, regulatory changes, and changing technologies e.g., the shift from internal combustion to electric power. Substantial investments are required to meet new technology outcomes, such as charging stations and renewable energy sources. Decarbonization represents a major shift in transport technologies that requires synchronized plans from both the transport and energy sectors as well as users and consumers if it is to be achieved in a timely manner.

17. Future support for transport in the CAREC region needs to emphasize countering the risks associated with the changing climate by both increasing the resilience of transport infrastructure and services, as well as supporting the shift to a low-carbon transport scenario by encouraging appropriate policies and plans as well as investments in low-carbon technologies and modes.

C. Economic Corridor and Smart Mobility

18. The CAREC corridors are well known as trade corridors linking major trade partners in East Asia, Europe, and elsewhere. The increasing utilization of digital technologies is transforming trade and transport services from what was largely the movement of goods from origin to destination to also incorporate logistics services covering the coordination and maintenance of the supply chain functions, including freight consolidation, storage, containerization, documentation, insurance, biosecurity and customs, and all other functions required to ensure the seamless multimodal movement of goods and services between points of origin to final destinations. These integrated logistics systems are increasingly important in the supply chain as the value and movement of goods increases and the role of transport services becomes an increasingly important component of the final product cost and quality.

Changes in the value chain are resulting in a more important role for the region's transport corridors as potential competitive routes emerge by land compared to the traditional low-cost maritime transport routes between East Asia and Europe.

The last decade has witnessed a rapid increase in the role of rail transport for higher value and time-sensitive manufactured products. The use of improved integrated logistics systems will increasingly become important in adding productivity to rail-based routes. Support for transport needs to extend beyond improvement of infrastructure, and an economic corridor approach is needed to include services and related components that will add value to services such as the provision of logistics centers, cold chain facilities, intermodal hubs, interchanges, and feeder access.[11] In addition, support services that cover vital trade facilitation components are needed to ensure economic corridors operate efficiently and effectively across borders and continents.

20. The transport sector is rapidly experiencing change as greater use is made of technological developments and innovations, including new business models and policies that contribute toward improved safety, efficiency, flexibility, integration, and environmental sustainability. So-called smart mobility solutions, such as intelligent transport systems, digitalization, low-emissions vehicles, public transport, shared mobility, cycling and nonmotorized transport, transport demand management, and integrated urban planning, can benefit transport along CAREC corridors, particularly at city nodes where increasing congestion adversely impacts long-distance freight movements. In addition, the transition toward the creation of green freight corridors and the role of urban nodes needs to be assessed and measures adopted to transform the sustainability of CAREC corridors.

D. Digitalization and Emerging Technologies

21. Digitalization is reshaping the transport sector, transforming transport and transport services over a wide spectrum, from engineering designs of infrastructure to the real-time scheduling and delivery of transport services. Emerging technologies—such as artificial intelligence, big data analytics, and intelligent transport systems—are set to become powerful enablers of efficiency and integration across all modes of transport in the CAREC region. These innovations hold significant potential to reduce trade and logistics costs, optimize asset utilization, and enhance the resilience of transport networks. To fully realize these benefits, it is crucial for the sector to embrace a forward-looking mindset open to advocating for new digital solutions and operational models. This technological shift is important for the region, where geographic distances and limited connectivity contribute considerably to the higher transport cost. By harnessing digital and artificial intelligence-driven approaches, the region can overcome these structural challenges, improve the competitiveness of trade corridors, and accelerate inclusive economic growth.

11 ADB. 2023. *Economic Corridor Development: From Conceptual Framework to Practical Implementation—Guidance Note*.

E. Regional Conflicts

22. Regional conflicts can have significant impact on international transport, and in recent years, the CAREC region has been affected by such events. Disruptions to existing transport routes result in higher costs associated with trade, forcing alternative routes to be sought and increasing transit times required to reach destinations. More recently, Russia's war in Ukraine and the conflict in the Red Sea have had a significant impact on trade by affecting routings and traditional patterns of trade and extending transit times and costs. The fast-growing rail services serving the East Asia–Europe trade were impacted by sanctions on the Russian Federation and some of this trade was diverted to the Corridor 2 route, which is constrained by capacity limitations at the Caspian Sea and many international borders and transshipment requirements. It has highlighted the need for greater route resilience by having alternative options for rerouting traffic. The sanctions on Russian trade have led to significant increases in trade using both Corridors 2 and 4 as traffic demand both shifts in route as well as supports increases in demand from new supplier origins.

23. Conflicts outside the region have also adversely impacted Central Asia directly and indirectly. Conflict in the Red Sea has affected trade and increased demand for land routes across Asia, including the demand for the use of CAREC corridors. The disruption to maritime routes goes beyond the direct impact on routes using the Red Sea, as increased transit times have a ripple effect, with shipping schedules on other routes disrupted as assets are operating longer voyage times, meaning global operations are impacted.

24. Dealing with unforeseen events requires additional resilience to be built into transport systems and operations to minimize the impacts of potential disruptions. This requires an assessment of the risks and identification of the costs of dealing with each risk factor. The results of such an assessment are likely to show that while some risks can be accommodated relatively easily others will be too costly to mitigate. The risks that are too costly to mitigate will instead require plans to cover anticipated disruptions to transport services.

Chapter IV

REVIEW OF THE CAREC TRANSPORT STRATEGY 2030

A. Overview

25. The CAREC Transport Strategy 2030 (CTS 2030) was prepared and endorsed by the CAREC ministers in 2019. Unlike its predecessor, the transport strategy was developed separately from the trade agenda, which was expected to provide a stronger alignment of all CAREC operational strategies toward achieving CAREC 2030. In this respect, the CTS was fully aligned with the objectives of reducing trade barriers and associated costs, increasing trade connectivity, and reducing trade turnover times. Within the CTS there are two individual modal transport strategies, one covering the railway sector and the other road safety (footnote 5). The MTR has broadly reviewed both these strategies to ensure that they remain relevant and continue to support the overall objectives of the transport sector.

26. The CAREC transport network consists of six multimodal corridors crossing the region broadly from east to west and north to south and represents the important trading routes serving the region for links to external markets as well as intra-CAREC routes serving individual countries. These routes were originally defined under the earlier Trade and Transport Strategy 2020 and were considered suitable and representative to continue supporting the economic and social development of the region. This review has not adjusted the corridor network given the technical and political challenges of route changes, and Map 1 illustrates the CAREC multimodal corridor network. However, the MTR suggests that a review of strategic needs, including the corridor alignments, will be required when considering the region's strategic transport requirements beyond 2030.

Map 1: CAREC Multimodal Corridors

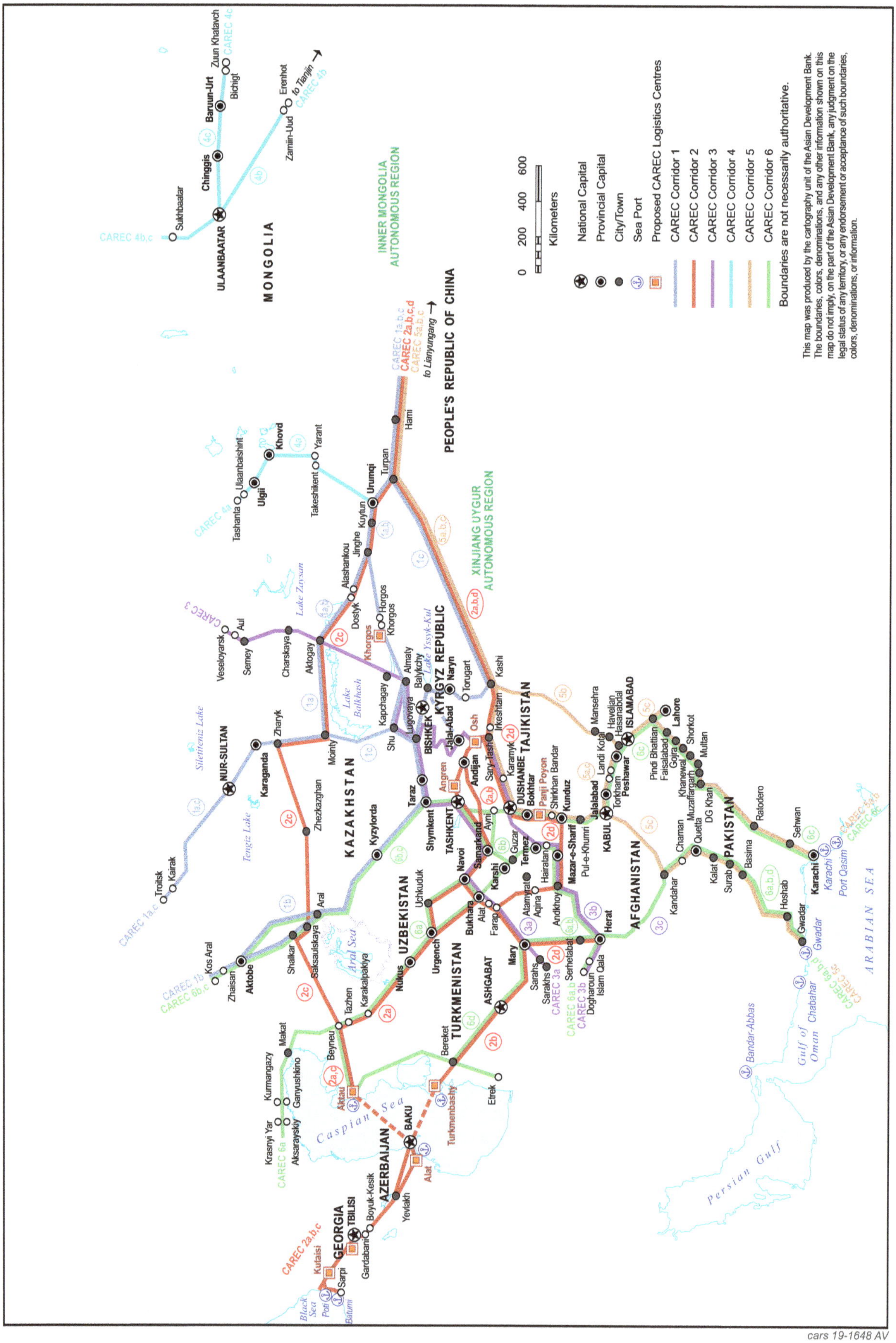

Source: ADB. 2020. *CAREC Transport Strategy 2030*.

B. Review of the Strategic Framework

27. The overall strategic framework was based on five key pillars covering (i) cross-border transport and logistics facilitation, (ii) roads and road asset management, (iii) road safety, (iv) railways, and (v) aviation. These pillars cover the bulk of most transport movements in the region, given that waterborne transport is relatively minor but an important link to multimodal connectivity, being focused to trans-Caspian trade and seaports in Georgia and Pakistan. The framework was also centered on achieving two primary objectives: connectivity and sustainability.

28. Consultations with agencies relevant to the transport and trade sector provided feedback on the overall strategic nature of the CTS 2030.[12] These discussions revealed that the strategic nature of the program provided important guidance and direction to each of the individual countries. In all countries, the CTS strategic framework provided a common focus to achieving improved connectivity. This was considered a crucial element for each of the countries given their landlocked geographical position and exceptional long distances to external markets. The focus on connectivity has underpinned the importance of the regional corridor network concept as a major development objective in national development plans. Prioritizing the improvement of national segments of the corridors has resulted in an improved and better-connected network overall. The resulting improved connectivity has had a substantive positive impact on each of the country's abilities to access both domestic markets as well as those beyond their national boundaries.[13] This outcome is well-aligned with the CAREC mission to establish "a regional cooperation platform to connect people, policies, and projects for shared and sustainable development." The resulting improved connectivity enables the corridors to facilitate increased people movement and trade throughout the region. The one area that has not yet received mainstream support, although its importance is well-recognized, concerns the delays attributable to border-crossing controls and procedures. This is discussed in paragraphs 33 to 39.

29. However, one aspect of the strategic framework that is not considered or reviewed is an assessment of how well the corridors perform. At the national level, corridors are reviewed largely as important national roads and few assessments are made of regional trade or impacts that occur beyond the national borders. In this respect, the constraints posed by inefficient and bureaucratic border-crossing processes and procedures are rarely examined as part of the transport requirements, and this has led to widespread problems at border crossing points (BCPs). Generally, portions of the corridor are selected for improvement or upgrading due to their deteriorated quality or limited

---

12 A core part of the MTR process involved conducting consultations with each CAREC country to obtain their feedback, ideas, issues, and recommendations on the appropriateness and relevance of the CAREC Transport Strategy 2030 (footnote 4).

13 ADB. 2023. *Evaluation of ADB Support for the Central Asia Regional Economic Cooperation Program, 2011–2022*.

capacity to handle increasing volumes of traffic, and feasibility studies are undertaken on a standalone basis to determine social needs and economic viability. An important element missing from the assessment is an overview of each corridor from a regional perspective, and it would be appropriate to undertake such reviews on a periodic basis to obtain an understanding of how individual corridors are performing and identify constraints that might impede future performance. This aspect is discussed further in the proposed recommendations section.

30. Transport infrastructure is perhaps a country's largest investment asset given its overall cost and widespread benefit to the national economy. This is mirrored in the overall support provided by the CAREC program to the transport sector, where $35.5 billion, representing 68% of total support, has been allocated to the sector since its inception until 2024 (Figure 1). It is therefore crucial that the values of the investments are retained through appropriate and adequately funded maintenance programs. To support this objective, the strategic framework placed priority on achieving sustainability and ensured that infrastructure continues to generate economic and social benefits over the long term. The MTR has identified the needs to incorporate improved maintenance as a primary thrust in all projects through a combination of different approaches. In some projects, direct support was provided to build the capacity of maintenance operations through the provision of maintenance equipment, capacity enhancement of maintenance staff, and resources to undertake increased maintenance activities. In some instances, enhancements of maintenance policies were implemented to increase the volume of maintenance activities through adoption of systems designed to increase resources and efficiencies specifically for maintenance purposes.

31. In addition to funding support, the CTS prioritized providing capacity building and knowledge management activities. Sustainability of infrastructure is not just the provision of adequate funds; it also requires knowledge of its design, maintenance, and management. To support this element of the program, resources were provided to support and deliver various capacity-building programs, as well as development and publication of knowledge products. The review of activities accomplished under the CTS revealed that a substantial number of workshops, training programs, and knowledge products were a major output during 2020–2024 (Appendix).

32. The focus on achieving connectivity, and sustainability in the transport sector are both important parameters and these objectives need to be continued through to 2030. Since the development of the CTS, greater awareness is being paid to dealing with unforeseen disasters triggered by natural hazards, changing climatic conditions, and geopolitical impacts. Disruptions to transport can cause significant costs to an economy, and it is increasingly recognized that the ability of infrastructure to withstand such adverse shocks is an important attribute and needs to be given priority. As mentioned in para. 15, the findings of the MTR suggest that resilience should be an added objective of the regional strategy.

C. Cross-Border Transport and Logistics Facilitation

33. Cross-border transport has remained a priority since the inception of the CAREC program, as the movement of people and goods between countries in the region, as well as to external destinations, has been a core objective of the program. However, delays at BCPs have been a key issue and have often been at a level that nullified the benefits attributable to vehicle time savings associated with connectivity improvements. The CAREC program initiated Corridor Performance Measurement and Monitoring (CPMM) in 2010 to specifically measure the delays and costs associated with traversing the important corridor BCPs in the region and identify critical bottlenecks and constraints associated with border crossings, particularly for freight traffic.[14]

34. Several investment projects were included in the CAREC program to address the BCP constraints. These projects, often referred to as Regional Improvement of Border Services Projects, have included components for both hard and soft infrastructure, since the physical capacity constraints associated with border facilities is only a part of the problem. Improvements to the soft side are equally critical as oftentimes the processes and procedures utilize legacy paper based systems that were originally designed to control rather than facilitate trade. Under CAREC's parallel trade strategy, the CITA 2030, measures have been established to enhance customs and other border control systems, such as sanitary and phytosanitary regulations and a variety of non-tariff barriers. An emphasis has been placed on transitioning from paper-based to electronic systems and ensuring that border systems adopt national single window systems that integrate and harmonize data from multiple government agencies to improve efficiency. As countries adopt digital electronic systems, it is also necessary for different country systems to communicate with each other to expedite processes across multiple borders, which is particularly important for exports beyond neighboring countries. For such systems to be effective and compatible, it is necessary for transport and trade agencies to collaborate closely to achieve improved trade and cross-border outcomes.

35. Evidence from CPMM indicates that reductions in border-crossing delays and costs over 2017–2023 are mixed, with positive outcomes for the road sector but not for rail-based transport. For road transport, the average time taken at a BCP has reduced from 16.9 hours in 2017 to 11 hours in 2023, while the cost has fallen from $159 to $131 (Figure 7). Exceptions for both parameters were experienced during the COVID-19 period, when time and cost delays increased. The CPMM data indicates that time and cost across all BCPs have reduced by more than 20%. However, the data also shows

[14] The CPMM tool was initiated in 2010 as part of the CAREC program's monitoring framework to measure the outcomes of CAREC investments in the transport network that focused on improving connectivity. The data is collected by private sector trucking companies and the reports prior to 2023 were published by ADB. Since then, responsibility for analysis and reporting has rested with the CAREC Institute, which is expected to continue with and further develop the methodology.

Figure 7: Indicators for CAREC Road and Railway Corridors, 2017–2023

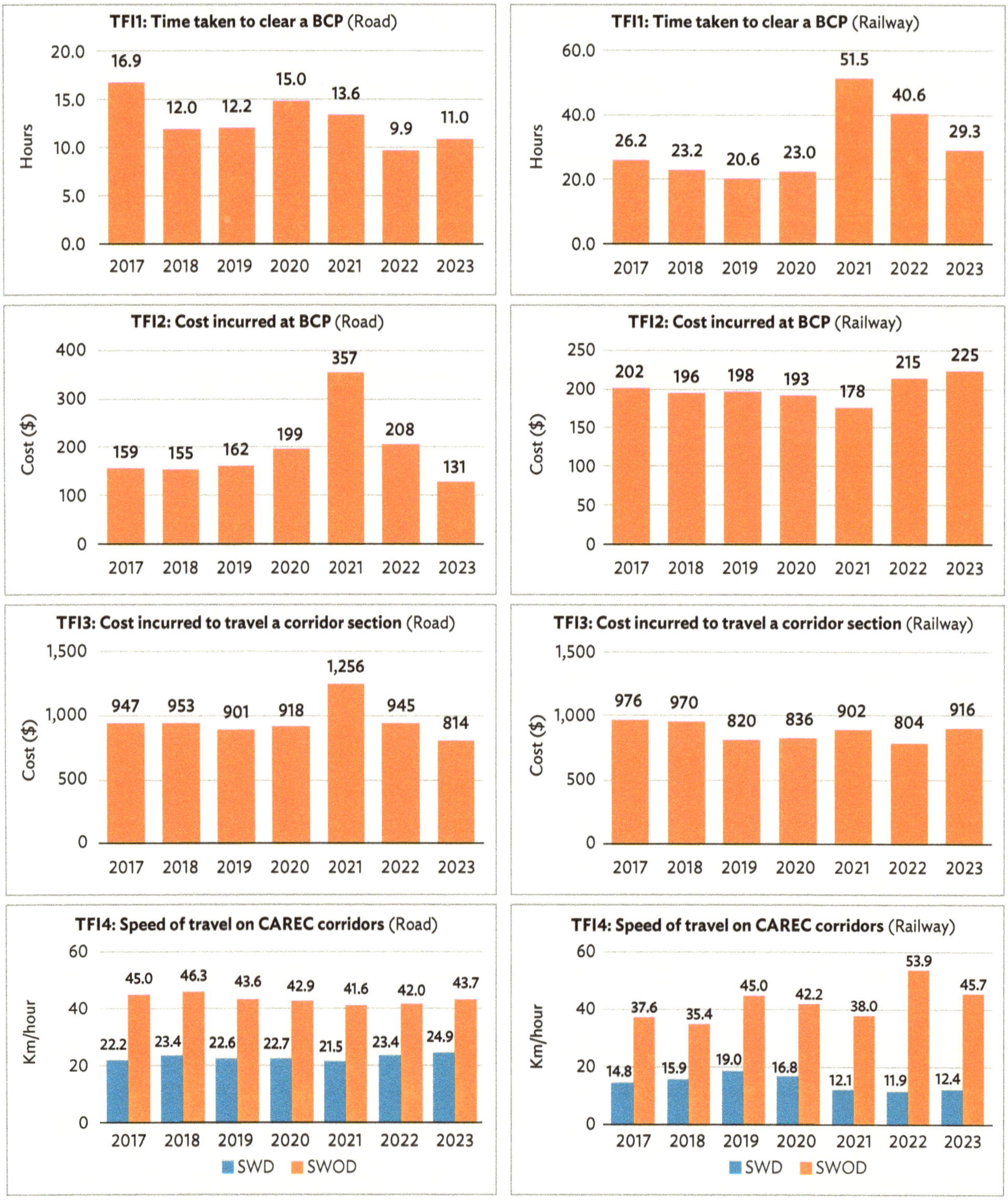

BCP = border crossing point, CAREC = Central Asia Regional Economic Cooperation, km/h = kilometers per hour, SWD = speed with delay, SWOD = speed without delay, TFI = trade facilitation indicator.
Source: CAREC Corridor Performance Measurement and Monitoring. Trade Facilitation Indicators (accessed 9 December 2025).

that at some important locations, time and delay are excessive and impact the overall regional results. Addressing these specific locations could significantly improve overall regional performance. With respect to railway border crossings, the results are less favorable, with time delays and costs marginally increasing between 2017 and 2023. While these regional parameters reflect the overall corridor network performance, there are large variations across the corridors, with many BCPs performing well and others experiencing excessive delays and costs. Therefore, it is advisable to prioritize addressing the BCPs with poor performance. Away from border crossings, road and railway corridor segments are performing well, reflecting substantial efforts by countries to improve road and rail connectivity. The trend in both road and rail costs indicates a downward movement, with reducing costs, while network speeds are broadly stable for roads but increasing for railway movements. Given the type of roads comprising the individual corridors, average speeds are unlikely to increase significantly in the future, especially since heavy trucks, some with trailers, are not expected to attain significantly higher speeds. Conversely, network speeds by rail continue to increase, and with further investment and improvements in railway infrastructure and technologies, future speeds are expected to continue an upward trend. This suggests that greater efforts should be given to railway improvements.

36. Investments have been implemented at several BCPs using both internal resources as well as external loans and grants. Despite the focus given to BCPs under the CTS, progress has been slow, especially given the large number of BCPs in the region that require investment and upgrading. The MTR concurs with the recommendations made by the independent evaluation of ADB support for the CAREC program (footnote 10) that "consideration should be given to scaling up the past experience of the Regional Improvement of Border Services projects so that the widespread delays and costs associated with border crossings can be reduced if not eliminated." Actions to expedite such a program are discussed in para. 58. Countries emphasized the need to reduce delays and costs at BCPs. Many have implemented national single window systems to speed up processing. Although improvements are still needed, there is a strong demand to enhance both physical and digital infrastructure at borders. The MTR notes that many border authorities are willing to invest in facilities to reduce times and costs for international business, and this should be prioritized in the CTS from 2026 to 2030.

37. The CAREC region has a long history in transit trade linking East Asia in the east with Europe in the west. In the past decade, this trade has grown substantially and has focused on developing railway routes as a potential alternative to the main maritime routes, particularly for higher value products where the shorter rail transit times offer keen competition. In comparison, maritime transport generally takes 28–40 days to link PRC ports with Europe, with container rates largely in the $1,500 to $2,000 band for a standard forty-foot container, while block container trains using the northern route from PRC through Kazakhstan, the Russian Federation, and Republic of Belarus to Europe reduce travel to 15–16 days with costs in the $2,800 to $3,200 range per

standard forty-foot container; Corridor 2 in comparison takes 16–21 days with costs in the $3,500 to $4,500 range.[15] Prior to 2022, the northern corridor volume of trade reached almost 1.5 million twenty-foot equivalent units (TEUs) a year and was an attractive alternative to maritime transport for various cargoes.[16] However, following the Russian invasion of Ukraine, the route through the Russian Federation was subject to constraints and many shippers opted to try alternative routes, the most popular of which was CAREC Corridor 2.[17] This multimodal corridor crosses Kazakhstan, the Caspian Sea, Azerbaijan, Georgia, and onward to Europe mostly either by train or a combination of ferry and train. There are also several route deviations or options, including those using portions of corridors in Turkmenistan and Uzbekistan. A further possible future sub-route linking to the corridor is the recently approved PRC–Kyrgyz Republic–Uzbekistan railway.

38. CAREC Corridor 2 is constrained by a combination of multiple border crossings, limitations on trans-Caspian shipping capacity, adverse marine navigable conditions, inefficient intermodal links between sea, rail, and road modes, the reduction in water depth of the Caspian Sea, and capacity limitations at Black Sea ports. Numerous assessments have been made of Corridor 2's potential.[18] These assessments have generally resulted in favorable recommendations subject to incorporating solutions for the aforementioned corridor constraints. The countries on the corridor all have expressed interest in unlocking the route's potential. Throughputs in trade on Corridor 2 increased considerably to 56,500 TEUs in 2024, suggesting that there is demand for the route despite the significant constraints posed by physical infrastructure and services and limited soft infrastructure border processes and procedures.[19] The consultations with countries conducted as part of the MTR highlighted the issues and potential demand for improved infrastructure and accompanying services, as well as countries' interests in developing the route. The MTR considers that there is potential scope for developing Corridor 2 route infrastructure and services to provide a competitive alternative option to the northern corridor, providing more transport options beyond the transit function to the individual countries of Central Asia. To enhance connectivity and boost competitiveness in the region, it is recommended to further support the development of Corridor 2 under the CTS during 2026–2030.

15 The comparative data is based on modified data from World Bank. 2023. *Middle Trade and Transport Corridor: Policies and Investments to Triple Freight Volumes and Halve Travel Time by 2030*. These costs are for illustrative purposes only and vary substantially based on port combinations.

16 The volume of 1.5 million TEUs also includes traffic between PRC and Russia; the estimated volume between PRC and Europe is at 618,000 TEUs.

17 Corridor 2 is referred to by several different titles in the literature, including the Middle Corridor, Transcaspian International Transport Route (TITR), and Trans-Caspian Transport Corridor (TCTC).

18 ADB. 2022. *CAREC Middle Corridor Assessment: Transport Connectivity on the Eurasian Transit Routes*; European Bank for Reconstruction and Development. 2023. *Sustainable Transport Connections between Europe and Central Asia;* World Bank. 2023. *Middle Trade and Transport Corridor: Policies and Investments to Triple Freight Volumes and Halve Travel Time by 2030*; and Organisation for Economic Co-operation Development. 2025 (forthcoming). *Enhancing the Competitiveness of the Trans-Caspian Transport Corridor (TCTC).*

19 This compares to 380,000 TEUs throughput on the Northern Corridor for common origin-destinations.

39. Investment support has prioritized transport infrastructure while the use of infrastructure, such as logistics, public transport, and tourism, has not been given much support in the CAREC program. This is unfortunate since the primary benefits from investment in infrastructure are gained from the use of the infrastructure through increased movement of people and goods and improved competitiveness. A review of investment documentation, particularly for road improvements, reveals that the studies that underpin the transport analysis largely omit important details about the use of the road infrastructure in terms of its contribution to regional trade and transport. There is limited information on the split between regional and domestic traffic, and the volumes and types of freight using the road corridors. Availability of information on the use of the road corridors, together with cross-border flows, could significantly contribute to the regional context of the investment and result in better quality regional assessments and impacts at project design, completion, and evaluation stages of the project cycle. The MTR suggests that such regional planning and assessment function be enhanced with improved data and regional transport models for assessing the regional coordination and integration aspects of the CAREC transport program and regional trade.

D. Roads and Road Asset Management

40. The road sector continues to be the sector receiving the greatest support, given the large backlog of roads that were in poor condition at the commencement of the CAREC program and the extensive impact of an improved road network in delivering economic and social development benefits. As noted earlier, the focus on delivering improved connectivity was also an important component of individual national transport plans and this common thread across CAREC countries provided the impetus to achieve a better-connected regional road network. The strategy recognized that a major issue in most countries was the risks associated with maintaining the road network in good condition, due to a combination of inefficient maintenance practices and insufficient funding allocations devoted to conducting maintenance activities. As a result, the strategy placed priority on strengthening road asset management practices and supporting policies to bolster the financing of road maintenance activities.

41. In most countries, road maintenance practices were based on legacy systems that assigned resources to resolve problems once they had become apparent. The change to more modern road asset management techniques shifts the focus to preventing roads from reaching a deteriorated state by predicting early road deterioration and allocating resources to maintain good quality pavements before deterioration sets in. Adopting and implementing such systems takes time and resources. Although good progress has been made in several countries, more time is required before road asset management systems are fully integrated into road operating agencies. Figure 8 illustrates the positive changes that have occurred in road asset management in many CAREC countries to date and indicates that it will take additional time before such practices are fully effective.

Figure 8: Road Asset Management Systems Maturity Assessment

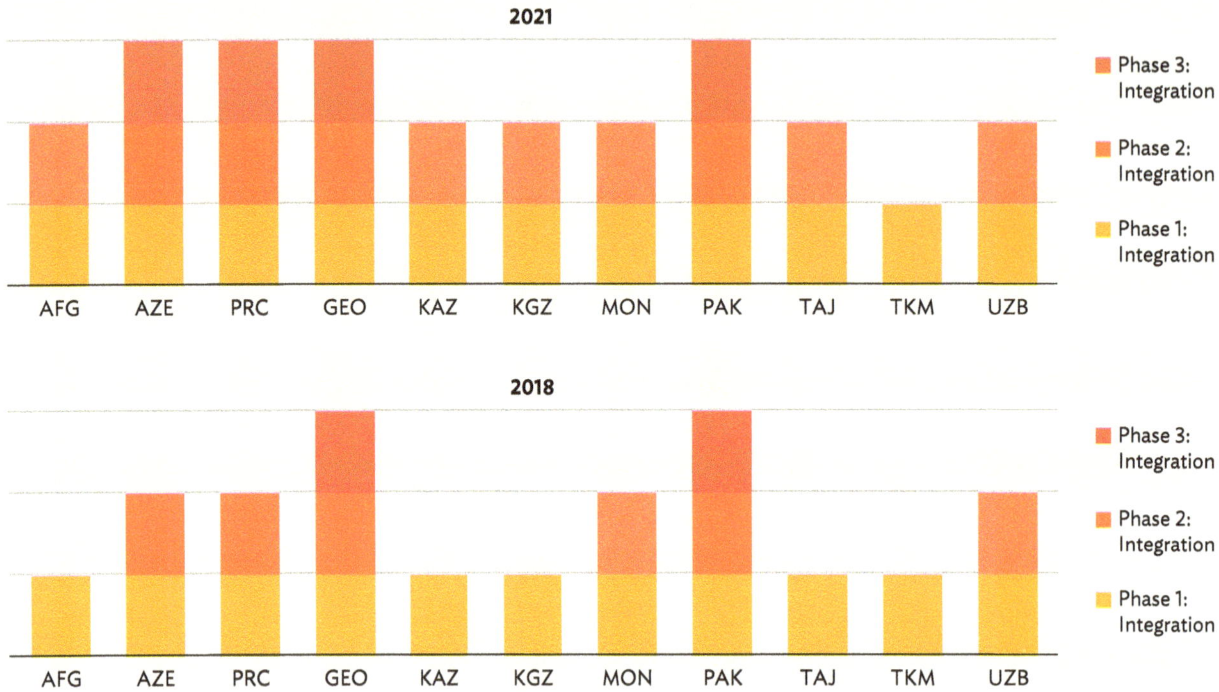

AFG = Afghanistan, AZE = Azerbaijan, PRC = People's Republic of China, GEO = Georgia, KAZ = Kazakhstan, KGZ = Kyrgyz Republic, MON = Mongolia, PAK = Pakistan, TAJ = Tajikistan, TKM = Turkmenistan, UZB = Uzbekistan.
Note: Solid shading means fully achieved, striped means partially achieved.
Source: ADB. 2021. *Road Asset Management Systems and Performace-based Road Maintenance Contracts in the CAREC Region*.

42. In parallel with road asset management, a significant related issue is the shortage of funds for road maintenance. Assessment of road financing policies revealed that in many countries the funds allocated for road maintenance are well below the required needs.[20] This is a serious problem given the volume of support invested in improving the CAREC corridors.

43. Given the high economic returns that are generated from effective road management, coupled with the priority programs discussed during country consultation, the MTR recommends that the strategy to achieve greater sustainability of the road networks through improved road asset management and financing should be continued as high priority.

[20] ADB. 2022. *Road Funds and Road User Charges in the CAREC Region*.

E. Road Safety

44. Road safety was identified as an important policy issue prior to adoption of the CTS and a separate CAREC road safety strategy was endorsed by the Ministerial Conference in 2016.[21] The basis of the strategy uses the "safe system approach" promulgated by the World Health Organization (WHO) and commonly used to achieve improvements in road safety outcomes. The strategy also has a focal target to reduce the number of deaths attributable to road crashes by 50% by 2030 compared to the base line level in 2010. This target is also in line with the WHO global target, which was also adopted by the United Nations Sustainable Development Goals. The MTR of the strategy indicates that the document remains valid and is consistent with global practices to reduce road crash deaths and injuries.

45. During consultations, the importance of addressing road safety was regularly mentioned by national agencies. However, despite the importance of reducing road crashes, most countries are experiencing difficulties in attaining the target reductions in road deaths. On the positive side, all countries have made good progress in reducing the number of fatalities compared to the 2010 baseline (Table). Several countries have reduced fatalities by over 30% although several countries have achieved less than 5% since the target was adopted. The overall picture suggests that a significantly greater effort is required between different agencies, particularly the police, highway agencies, and health authorities, if the 2030 target is to be realized. The statistics also indicate that official police records significantly underestimate the likely number of fatalities as estimated by the WHO. Underestimation decreases the importance of the road safety problem and undervalues the economic losses attributable to road crashes.

46. A review of the national road safety performance indicators presented in the latest WHO status report clearly indicates that CAREC countries need to strengthen various actions to achieve better road safety outcomes.[22] For instance, several countries either do not have a national road safety strategy to guide actions necessary to reduce fatalities and injuries, and only two countries have indicated that their action plans are fully funded. The absence of specific funding for road safety is a global issue and in many CAREC countries progress in reducing road crashes is impeded by limited resource availability. Good progress has been achieved in promoting safer roads in investment projects, and all countries are now incorporating road safety audit techniques and star ratings that result in safer road infrastructure outcomes. This progress needs to be accelerated by adopting a programmatic rather than project approach to safer roads, simply because the project approach restricts improvements to the limited length of a road under a project, rather than impacting the thousands of kilometers of roads comprising the network. This change in approach could scale up the impact of safer roads.

[21] ADB. 2016. *Safely Connected: A Regional Road Safety Strategy for CAREC Countries, 2017–2023.*

[22] WHO. 2023. *Global Status Report on Road Safety 2023.*

CAREC Road Safety Progress, 2010–2021
(Number of fatalities)

Country	Based on Official Police Records			WHO Estimates		Fatalities Reduction[a] (%)
	2010	2016	2021	2016	2021	
Azerbaijan	925	759	706	2,096	1,769	23.7
People's Republic of China	65,225	58,022	62,218	256,180	248,099	4.6
Georgia	685	581	449	621	476	34.5
Kazakhstan	3,379	2,625	2,270	2,910	2,340	32.8
Kyrgyz Republic	875	812	869	1,069	869	0.7
Mongolia	491	484	383	494	414	22.0
Pakistan	5,192	4,448	5,816	27,543	27,568	12.0
Tajikistan	411	427	395	1,622	1,352	3.9
Turkmenistan	NA	NA	NA	NA	NA	
Uzbekistan	2,731	2,496	2,197	3,040	3,155	19.6

CAREC = Central Asia Regional Economic Cooperation, NA = not available, WHO = World Health Organization.
[a] Based on Official Police Records 2010 to 2021.
Source: WHO Global Road Safety Status Reports (various years).

47. During 2020–2024, the CTS allocated considerable attention to promoting road safety through an extensive program of training workshops and publication of knowledge products. The knowledge products are considered valuable for promoting new and different techniques and the reports are widely known in the region. The focus on road safety audit, use, and application of star ratings, attention to infrastructure for pedestrians, and managing road worksites have all contributed to improved knowledge about safer road infrastructure, and such measures are now being widely adopted by highway agencies. In some cases, such as amending design changes to improve safety, adoption takes time as institutional adjustments require acceptance in several different agencies. Overall, the MTR considers that the capacity building and knowledge activities of the CTS have been successful in raising awareness in road safety, especially in highway agencies. Future activities should extend the capacity building to other agencies, particularly enforcement agencies, and build bridges between the police and other agencies to achieve greater coordination and cooperation between different agencies, which commonly operate in separate silos.

48. The general conclusion from the MTR assessment of road safety is that the CAREC region has achieved significant progress in road safety outcomes, but greater efforts need to be sustained if desired targets are to be achieved. In particular, countries need to allocate greater attention to preparing multisectoral road safety plans and ensure that such plans are adequately funded and implemented. Policies supporting greater safety outcomes need to be strengthened and enforced. The greater use of digital technologies can improve the effectiveness of safety

projects and programs, as well as strengthen enforcement. During the 2026–2030 period, greater consideration needs to be provided to shift the focus from knowledge sharing to action by implementing road safety projects and programs designed to widen the scale of road safety outcomes and achieve greater development impact.

F. Railways

49. Initiatives in the railway sector have been guided by the CAREC railway strategy approved in 2017 (footnote 5). This strategy has provided an appropriate framework to develop the region's railway systems. The strategy proposed actions be focused on a combination of three key outputs: (i) improved railway infrastructure, (ii) increased robust commercial capabilities, and (iii) improved legal and regulatory frameworks. Baseline indicators for each of these outputs were quantified under the strategy's results-based framework.[23] To help define the physical infrastructure needs across the region, the strategy identified six Designated Railway Corridors (Map 2) and prepared a methodology for prioritizing individual investment projects.

50. A review of the strategy suggests that the broad thrust remains valid, with a continuing need to support the three priorities, which remain to be attained in national railway systems. It would be appropriate to measure the relative progress of each of the output indicators specified in the results-based framework to ascertain their interim status. Amendments and corrective actions can then be taken to achieve or adjust the milestones as appropriate.

51. The work under the railway theme is conducted under the auspices of the leadership of the Railway Working Group. Established in 2014, it has met regularly and minutes of these meetings indicate that it helps to identify and facilitate the annual sector work program as provided under the CAREC Railway Sector Development technical assistance program.[24] This program facilitates studies and other support activities to assist member country railways in implementing elements of the CAREC Railway Strategy 2030. A significant contribution to the regional railway strategy was a study that conducted a regional assessment of railways in the CAREC region.[25] This provides an overall assessment of the region's rail corridors, reviews its institutions and policies, estimates traffic and operational performance, and examines possible options for introducing greater commercial practices. This seminal study provides a framework for potential future assistance.

23 ADB. 2017. *CAREC Railway Strategy, 2017–2030*. Appendix 1.

24 The ninth meeting of the Railway Working Group was held on 10-12 June 2025 in Bishkek, Kyrgyz Republic.

25 ADB. 2022. *The Situation of Railways in CAREC Countries and Opportunities for Investment, Commercialization and Reform*.

Map 2: CAREC Designated Railway Corridors

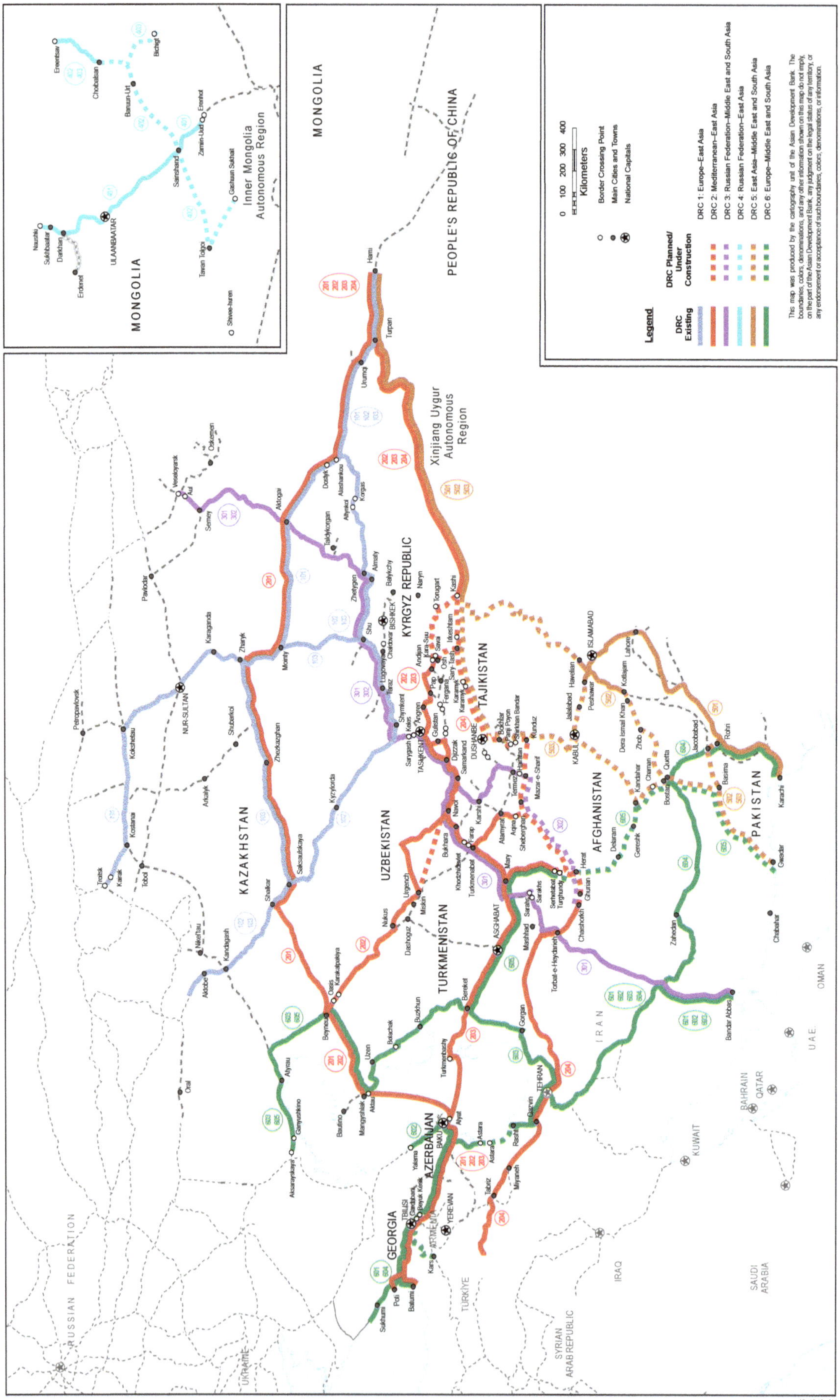

Source: ADB. 2017. *CAREC Railway Strategy, 2017–2030*.

52. In the remaining strategy period of 2026–2030, the CAREC railway subsector activities will largely focus on the potential for increasing the competitiveness of Corridor 2 (paras. 37 and 38). The potential of this corridor will be underpinned by the East Asia–Europe trade, the bulk of which will utilize containerized rail transport. Other work themes are expected to include the digitalization of railway operations and sector management, increased port–rail connectivity, technologies to enhance decarbonization and promote sustainability of railway operations, and assessment of risks posed by climate change and potential disaster events. The railway subsector will also need to improve facilities, processes, and procedures associated with BCPs (paras. 34 and 35).

G. Aviation

53. Aviation is important to the CAREC region given the vast distances between national capitals and remote locations and especially to countries outside the landlocked region. Although air transport is important, it has not received priority in terms of its development, and travel between the region's capital cities is often difficult, with few direct links, and this is repeated for travel to destinations outside the region. In many countries initiating reforms has been slow and this has retarded the growth of the airline industry and impeded business development and trade. Important constraints concern limited competition and restricted market access, and this is encouraged by the regulatory framework.

54. The CTS included the aviation sector after an initial scoping study that recommended a strategic framework for the sector. This study highlighted the crucial role of aviation in facilitating connectivity in an environment where aviation played an increasingly important role in facilitating business activities and developing key sectors such as tourism. The early years covered by the CTS were affected by the COVID-19 pandemic, which had a devastating impact on the aviation sector through the restricted movement of people around the world. However, following the lifting of pandemic restrictions, the civil aviation sector has witnessed a boom in demand, and the region has experienced a significant upward shift in aircraft and people movements, both within the region as well as to and from the region. In 2024, passenger capacity offered on many routes was 50% above those recorded in 2019. The increase in demand covers a wide range of connections including those with the PRC, Europe, the Russian Federation, Türkiye, as well as within the CAREC region.

55. The dynamic changes in the region's demand for aviation services have led to significant growth in aviation infrastructure, particularly investment in airport terminals. A considerable portion of investment has been undertaken by the private sector through public–private partnership agreements. Engaging the private sector has had positive impacts in terms of increasing efficiency and improving service levels. In the remaining CTS period, activities in the aviation sector are likely to center upon

supporting public sector priorities, such as guiding regulatory policy and supporting aviation strategies and also exploring the potential for supporting aviation expansion through private sector initiatives. The continued emphasis on training and capacity building and the delivery of webinars and seminars based on demand, together with the implementation of studies and assessments on priority topics, is expected to comprise the core activities of the aviation sector. The country consultations conducted as part of this MTR exercise confirmed that the aviation strategy of the CTS is appropriate and should be continued during the period to 2030.

Chapter V

RECOMMENDATIONS OF THE MIDTERM REVIEW

A. Introduction

56. The recommendations of the MTR are largely based on consultations with stakeholders at the country level and particularly feedback received during workshops with national authorities (footnote 4). As noted earlier, the MTR was carried out jointly with the MTRs of the CITA 2030 and the CAREC Digital Strategy 2030, and this enhanced the integration of these relevant strategies, both of which are vital to transport development in the region.

B. Effectiveness of the Existing CTS 2030

57. The CTS 2030 has successfully delivered improvements in connectivity and sustainability in the transport sector and largely continues to be relevant. However, it needs to reflect the rapidly changing regional landscape and incorporate emerging and innovative technologies that are having a significant impact on the delivery of transport infrastructure and services. Transport corridors can unlock greater potential by transforming infrastructure into economic corridors. This can be done by enhancing mobility and feeder access, integrating trade facilitation and digitalization measures, and supporting logistics, tourism, and other economic activities along a corridor's area of influence. In this respect, the MTR concludes that the overall effectiveness of the corridors can be enhanced by a combination of actions that will strengthen cross-border transport and increase corridor efficiency, promote modal diversification together with integration of logistics systems and greater use of smart mobility systems, scale up digitalization and expand resilient, safe, and clean transport, and deepen institutional collaboration and planning systems. Actions in each of these areas are described below.

C. Strengthening Cross-Border Transport and Corridor Efficiency

58. The strengthening of cross-border transport and improved corridor efficiency can enhance regional trade and connectivity across the CAREC region by:

(i) Establishing a dedicated financing facility for the improvement and digitalization of BCPs covering infrastructure as well as processes and procedures through harmonized and digitalized permissions and inspections, preferably on both sides of the border, and where possible simultaneously;

(ii) Expanding corridor-based coordinated border management, harmonized digital customs systems, and mutual recognition of inspection and certification procedures to more BCPs;

(iii) Explicitly linking the BCP improvements to faster customs clearance, reduced trade costs, and standardized data exchange (e.g., single window systems, paperless trade initiatives);

(iv) Promoting an economic corridor approach to comprehensively address transport connectivity, accessibility, and mobility; remove bottlenecks; and enhance economic activities along corridors (e.g., multimodal logistic centers, dry ports, economic free zones, tourism);

(v) Enhancing capacity and connectivity along CAREC corridors, especially Corridor 2, through a combination of infrastructure upgrades, operation of multimodal logistics hubs and dry ports, better harmonized regulations, introduction of competition-enhancing reforms, and improved digital processes;[26]

(vi) Addressing critical capacity bottlenecks in Caspian Sea transport by expanding port capacity, modernizing fleets to increase shipping capacity and operating efficiency, and addressing risks of port operational performance and safe navigation due to reduced water levels; and

(vii) Addressing future demand pressures and redundancy options for Black Sea ports by expanding port capacity and delivering efficient multimodal access.

[26] CAREC Corridor 2 largely coincides with the Middle Corridor.

D. Promoting Increased Modal Diversification, Integrated Logistics Systems, and Smart Mobility

59. There is a general requirement to diversify modal connectivity and enhance resilient and sustainable transport systems, which can be promoted by providing greater opportunities for using alternative modes of transport, integrating logistics systems, and utilizing smart mobility options. This can be achieved by:

(i) Supporting all modes of transport (road, railway, aviation, and waterborne) ensuring their balanced development, modernization, and mutual integration to sustainably and resiliently serve the region's transport needs;

(ii) Strengthening intermodal connectivity, especially among ports, railways, and roads to boost efficiency and lower logistics costs;

(iii) Encouraging policy frameworks that support modal shift to low-carbon transport options, such as railway and waterborne transport, and promoting greater collaboration with energy and other sector activities;

(iv) Supporting investments and capacity enhancement in waterborne transport, including Caspian Sea shipping and inland waterway systems;

(v) Assisting with harmonization of logistics processes and proposing regional standards for multimodal documentation (e.g., digital waybills, multimodal freight manifests) that also link to international documentation standards and systems;

(vi) Highlighting the importance of unified corridor performance monitoring, tying logistics efficiency directly to trade competitiveness; and

(vii) Promoting intelligent transport systems, transport digitalization, e-mobility, comprehensive public transport development, and sustainable urban planning to achieve more efficient ways of moving people and goods, and to remove bottlenecks along the corridors through the newly created Smart Mobility Working Group.

E. Scaling Up Green, Resilient, Inclusive, and Digitalized Transport

60. Global developments have highlighted the magnitude of the transport sector's contributions to adversely affecting sustainability and the climate, and it is important that activities in the transport sector closely align with programs and targets established by CAREC countries. In order to better align with these targets, the transport sector needs to scale up its activities to promote green, resilient, and digitized transport across the region by:

(i) Including resilience (infrastructure, institutions, and operations) as one of the strategic objectives of the CTS 2030 alongside connectivity and sustainability;

(ii) Enhancing further use of greener modes of transport such as railways and waterborne transport while supporting greening and electrification of other modes of transport (e.g., promotion of the Green Roads Tool Kit and Green Ports Tool Kit) and creating low-emissions zones in urban areas supporting carbon emission targets to support nationally determined contributions;

(iii) Supporting harmonization of technical standards to ensure consistent road-bearing capacity, safety compliance, climate resilience, and use of sustainable low-carbon materials across CAREC countries;

(iv) Broadening road safety efforts by adopting the safe system approach and enhancing digital solutions—including safer vehicles, safer behavior, better post-crash care, and improved institutional road safety management;

(v) Utilizing the CAREC Climate and Sustainability Project Preparatory Fund and other resources for the preparation of digitally enabled, green, and resilient transport projects;

(vi) Incorporating green trade corridors and green customs tool as part of the CAREC corridor network—e.g., promote sustainable logistics practices especially for international freight operators;

(vii) Developing CAREC Corridor Digital Trade and Transit Platforms to integrate BCPs, logistics, and customs processes; and

(viii) Integrating trade-related digital platforms (such as cargo tracking, e-customs, and green customs tools[27]) as part of transport projects.

---

27 Green customs tools are customs procedures, technologies, and capacities that support environmental objectives. They strengthen control of environmentally sensitive goods, help enforce multilateral environmental agreements, and enable climate-friendly trade practices. In the CAREC context, these tools align with sustainable trade facilitation measures such as digitalization, advanced risk management, and paperless trade processes that make border operations more efficient while reducing environmental footprint.

F. Deepening Institutional Collaboration and Future Planning

61. To ensure long-term and coordinated transport development from a regional perspective it is necessary to develop a region-focused transport model to evaluate and measure impacts of investments in, and policies applied to, CAREC corridors covering all modes. Measures proposed to support the deepening of institutional collaboration and future planning are:

(i) Enhancing the CAREC Institute's planning and advisory functions by creating a dedicated transport and logistics center with functions on transport and economic corridor planning, policy advice, and capacity building by initially scaling up the current functions of the CAREC CPMM;

(ii) Expanding monitoring mechanisms such as CPMM and encouraging the use of time release surveys and key performance indicators at BCPs to assess delays and drive improvements;

(iii) Revising institutional structures of the Transport Sector Coordinating Committee and its working groups to reflect emerging priorities and enable a more adaptive and inclusive approach to regional planning;

(iv) Establishing a Smart Mobility Working Group and Road Working Group and continue regular activities of the Railway Working Group under the Transport Sector Coordinating Committee to monitor the CTS MTR and other CAREC transport outputs and outcomes (Figure 9);

(v) Strengthening the link between transport and trade facilitation bodies and enhancing the coordination with the relevant committees and working groups on both the CITA and CAREC Digital Strategies by jointly organizing transport and trade working groups for synchronized policy and project planning;

(vi) Involving the private sector (e.g., freight forwarders, logistics companies) to help drive both transport and trade facilitation activities and results;

(vii) Preparing annual regional-focused transport sector profile and flagship thematic assessment reports focusing on aspects of CAREC countries' transport needs utilizing Asian Transport Observatory and CPMM in collaboration with the CAREC Institute and other partners;

(viii) Supporting the adoption of CAREC-wide trade and transport facilitation committees at national and regional levels;

Figure 9: Proposed Structure of Transport Sector Coordinating Committee and Working Groups

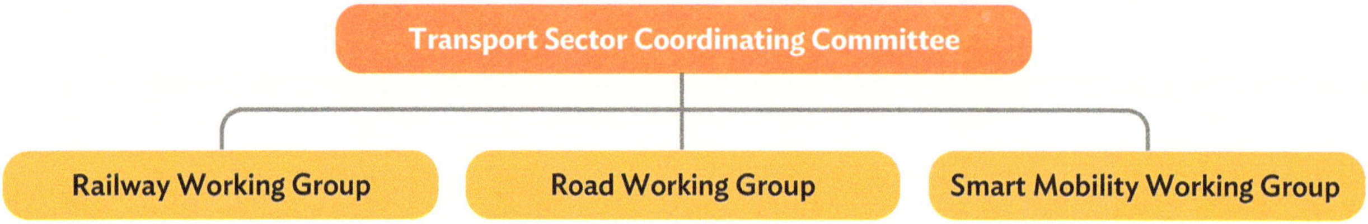

Source: Asian Development Bank.

(ix) Continuing efforts for supporting and strengthening capacity development and knowledge partnerships with the CAREC Institute and other institutions; and

(x) Reflecting on strategic needs beyond 2030, including evolving trade patterns, climate risks, and potential technological disruption.

G. Continuing Support for Capacity Building and Knowledge Products

62. A core component of CTS 2030 has been the focus on capacity building, training programs, and knowledge products. This element of the strategy has been particularly strong in the road asset management and road safety spheres, with the delivery of many training programs and knowledge publications, but has also involved several training events and knowledge publications in railways, cross-border transport, and aviation (Appendix). It is recommended that CTS 2030 continue its support to build capacity in needed technical areas, which require expanding to cover advances in technical and digital technologies. Collaboration with and learning from the experiences and lessons from other subregional programs such as the Greater Mekong Subregion Program and South Asia Subregional Economic Cooperation will also be beneficial. Technologies are expanding rapidly and are likely to have significant outcomes and impacts on developments in the transport sector.

H. Enhancing the Role of the CAREC Institute

63. The MTR recommends that the CAREC Institute take on an increasing role in the development of the region's transport sector through undertaking important technical studies, research, and assessments that would contribute toward achieving the strategy. This has partially commenced through its more active role in the CPMM to strengthen its policy analytics and advocacy and needs to be expanded to cover additional priority activities. Several other potential areas could be supported by the CAREC Institute, but this would depend on the recruitment of transport researchers, the technical skills of the transport team, and the approved work program.[28]

I. Strategic Needs Beyond 2030

64. Before the end of the CTS 2030 period, efforts will be required to assess the transport needs of the region beyond 2030. This work will be based on the transport planning and modelling activities that are recommended as part of the CTS 2030 program to provide oversight of the operations of the individual transport corridors, as well as support the monitoring program. It should assess the validity of the current corridor network and determine if additions and adjustments are required based on the increasing demand for movement in the region for the future time period of the new strategy. The assessment should also focus on improving the intermodal movements of goods and people.

[28] The following is an interim list of potential technical activities that could be undertaken by the CAREC Institute to augment knowledge of the transport sector in the CAREC region: (i) further strengthening of the CPMM annual report publications; (ii) study of logistics operations in CAREC countries utilizing the containerization study conducted in 2024–2025; (iii) inputs to the transport model to be developed for monitoring of freight flows and development of CAREC corridors; (iv) support to the transport leadership program for the CAREC countries; and (vi) development of data and information platform for the CAREC region utilizing the Asian Transport Observatory.

Appendix

WORKSHOPS, TRAINING PROGRAMS, AND KNOWLEDGE PRODUCTS, JANUARY 2020–JUNE 2025

Title of Publication/Event	Date
January 2020–June 2021	
A. Overall Transport	
19th CAREC Senior Officials Meeting—Transport Session	October 2020
2019 CAREC Transport Sector Annual Report	October 2020
B. Cross-Border Transport and Logistics	
CAREC Webinar series—Ports and Logistics (Two sessions)	February 2021
Ports and Logistics Scoping Study in CAREC Countries Volume 1	March 2021
Ports and Logistics Scoping Study in CAREC Countries Volume II	March 2021
C. Roads and Road Asset Management	
Tajikistan—Training Program on RAMS and PBC	February 2020
Online Course on Basic Road Construction for Non-Engineers (13 modules)	August 2020
RAM and RAMS Virtual Workshop (in collaboration with CAREC Institute)	August 2020
Afghanistan—RAMS and PBC Training (Three sessions)	February–March 2021
RAM Workshop on CAREC Maturity Assessment and Training of Trainers (in collaboration with CAREC Institute)	March 2021
Kyrgyz Republic—RAMS and PBC Training Workshop	June 2021
D. Road Safety	
Mongolia—National Training Workshops on Road Safety Engineering (in collaboration with CAREC Institute)	May 2020
CAREC Road Safety Engineering Manual 4: Pedestrian Safety	February 2021
E. Railways	
Track Capacity and Timetabling Software	May 2020
CAREC Railway Working Group Newsletter	December 2020
Railway Sector Assessment for Afghanistan	March 2021
Railway Sector Assessment for Azerbaijan	March 2021
Railway Sector Assessment for the PRC	March 2021
Railway Sector Assessment for Georgia	March 2021
Railway Sector Assessment for Kazakhstan	March 2021

continued on next page

Table *continued*

Title of Publication/Event	Date
Railway Sector Assessment for Kyrgyz Republic	March 2021
Railway Sector Assessment for Mongolia	March 2021
Railway Sector Assessment for Pakistan	March 2021
Railway Sector Assessment for Tajikistan	March 2021
Railway Sector Assessment for Turkmenistan	March 2021
Railway Sector Assessment for Uzbekistan	March 2021
F. Aviation	
Impact of COVID-19 on CAREC Aviation and Tourism	November 2020
Blog: Five ways to Revitalize Aviation and Tourism in Central Asia	November 2020
CAREC Webinar Series: Aviation and Tourism (Three sessions)	January–March 2021
July 2021–June 2022	
A. Overall Transport	
2020 CAREC Transport Annual Report (Abridged online version)	October 2021
CAREC Transport Sector Progress Report and Work Plan (July 2020 to August 2021)	October 2021
B. Roads and Road Asset Management	
Knowledge-Sharing Workshop on RAMS (Georgia, Pakistan, and Tajikistan)	October 2021
Workshop: RAMS and Performance-Based Road Maintenance Contracts (Afghanistan)	March 2021
Workshop: RAMS and Performance-Based Road Maintenance Contracts (Kyrgyz Republic)	June 2021
RAMS and Performance-Based Road Maintenance Contracts in the CAREC Region (English and Russian versions)	November 2021
C. Road Safety	
Road Safety Engineering: Star Ratings for Road Safety Audits Online Workshop	November 2021
Uzbekistan—Crash Investigation Training	December 2021
Kyrgyz Republic—Crash Investigation Training	January 2022
Turkmenistan—Road Safety Engineering Workshop*	April 2022
Kyrgyz Republic—Online Training on the Road Safety Problem	April 2022
Pedestrian Safety Training in CAREC Countries	June 2022
CAREC Road Safety Engineering Manual 5—Star Ratings for Road Safety Audit	June 2022
D. Railways	
The Situation of Railways in CAREC Countries and Opportunities for Investment, Commercialization, and Reform (English and Russian versions)	April 2022
July 2022–June 2023	
A. Overall Transport	
19th CAREC Transport Sector Coordinating Committee Meeting	October 2022
2022 CAREC Transport Sector Progress Report and Work Plan	October 2022
20th Transport Sector Coordinating Committee Meeting	May 2023
2023 CAREC Transport Sector Progress Report and Work Plan	June 2023

continued on next page

Table *continued*

Title of Publication/Event	Date
B. Cross-Border Transport and Logistics	
Developers Guide to Planning and Design of Logistic Centers in CAREC Countries	April 2023
C. Roads and Road Asset Management	
Road Funds and Road User Charges in the CAREC Region	December 2022
D. Road Safety	
Road Safety Report Card for the CAREC Region	July 2022
Mongolia—Crash Investigation Training	March 2023
Tajikistan—Crash Investigation Training	March 2023
E. Railways	
6th Railway Working Group Meeting	October 2022
7th Railway Working Group Meeting	May 2023
July 2023–June 2024	
A. Overall Transport	
21st Transport Sector Coordinating Committee Meeting	April 2024
2024 CAREC Transport Sector Progress Report and Work Plan	June 2024
B. Cross Border Transport and Logistics	
Middle Corridor Initial Assessment Report	May 2023
C. Roads and Road Asset Management	
CAREC Highways Workshop	May 2023
Performance-Based Road Maintenance Contracts in the CAREC Region	December 2023
D. Road Safety	
CAREC Road Safety Engineering Manual 6: Identifying, Investigating, and Treating Blackspots	May 2024
Road Crash Data Review and Reporting—Training on Improvement to Crash Data Management	June 2024
E. Railways	
Eighth Railway Working Group Meeting	May 2024
F. Aviation	
Low-Cost Carrier Opportunities, Air Transport Liberalization, and Post-Pandemic Recovery in CAREC	September 2023
Air Cargo Report	February 2024
July 2024–June 2025	
A. Overall Transport	
Country Consultation on MTR of CTS 2030 and Workshop in Mongolia	February 2025
CAREC National Focal Point Retreat and CTS 2030 MTR Discussion	March 2025
Country Consultation on CTS 2030 MTR and Workshop in the PRC (combined with a workshop on the next country partnership strategy workshop)	March 2025

continued on next page

Table *continued*

Title of Publication/Event	Date
Country Consultation on CTS 2030 MTR and Workshop in Azerbaijan	April 2025
Country Consultation on CTS 2030 MTR and Workshop in the Kyrgyz Republic	April 2025
Country Consultation on CTS 2030 MTR and Workshop in Uzbekistan	April 2025
Country Consultation on CTS 2030 MTR and Workshop in Tajikistan	April 2025
Country Consultation on CTS 2030 MTR and Workshop with Georgia (virtual)	May 2025
Country Consultation on CTS 2030 MTR and Workshop with Turkmenistan (virtual)	May 2025
Side event on CTS 2030 MTR at the 2025 Summit of International Transport Forum	May 2025
Country Consultation on CTS 2030 MTR and Workshop in Pakistan (in collaboration with CAREC Institute)	May 2025
22nd Transport Sector Coordinating Committee Meeting	June 2025
2024 CAREC Transport Sector Progress Report and Work Plan	June 2025
B. Road Safety	
CAREC Road Safety Engineering Manual 7: Why and How to Manage Speed	August 2024
APRSO Annual Meeting and Study Tour (Kyrgyz Republic, Mongolia, Uzbekistan)	October 2024
CAREC Road Crash Investigation Manual	March 2025
Azerbaijan Road Crash Data Review and Reporting: Status and Recommendations	March 2025
Georgia Road Crash Data Review and Reporting: Status and Recommendations	March 2025
Kazakhstan Road Crash Data Review and Reporting: Status and Recommendations	March 2025
Kyrgyz Republic Road Crash Data Review and Reporting: Status and Recommendations	March 2025
Mongolia Road Crash Data Review and Reporting: Status and Recommendations	March 2025
Pakistan Road Crash Data Review and Reporting: Status and Recommendations	March 2025
Tajikistan Road Crash Data Review and Reporting: Status and Recommendations	March 2025
Uzbekistan Road Crash Data Review and Reporting: Status and Recommendations	March 2025
APRSO and CAREC Road Safety Capacity Building Program—Webinar Series	March–May 2025
Two Trainings on Road Safety Knowledge for Mongolia	March 2025
Interactions Between Climate and Road Safety Measures in the CAREC Region—*ADB Sustainable Development Working Paper Series* (No. 107)	June 2025
C. Railways	
Ninth Railway Working Group Meeting	June 2025

APRSO = Asia Pacific Road Safety Observatory, CAREC = Central Asia Regional Economic Cooperation, COVID-19 = coronavirus disease, CTS = CAREC Transport Strategy, MTR = midterm review, PBC = performance-based contracting, PRC = People's Republic of China, RAM = road asset management, RAMS = road asset management system.

* With CAREC Institute.

Source: CAREC Secretariat.

www.ingramcontent.com/pod-product-compliance
Lightning Source LLC
Chambersburg PA
CBHW041800220926
51847CB00014B/264
* 9 7 8 9 2 9 2 7 7 6 8 4 8 *